10 STEPS TO CREATE A BRAND

Start-up Edition

Alex Williams

Copyright © 2024 Alex Williams Design

All rights reserved. No parts of this book may be reproduced without written permission.

CONTENTS

Title Page
Copyright
Introduction
Chapter 1 – Naming Your Brand　　　　　　　　　　1
Chapter 2 – Brand Personality　　　　　　　　　　　7
Chapter 3 – Brand Values, Mission and Vision　　　15
Chapter 4 – Target Audience　　　　　　　　　　　19
Chapter 5 – Services/Products　　　　　　　　　　23
Chapter 6 – Visual Identity　　　　　　　　　　　　29
Chapter 7 – Consistency　　　　　　　　　　　　　38
Chapter 8 – Claiming Your Space　　　　　　　　　42
Chapter 9 – Marketing　　　　　　　　　　　　　　45
Chapter 10 – Customer Service　　　　　　　　　　55
Summary　　　　　　　　　　　　　　　　　　　　61
Checklist　　　　　　　　　　　　　　　　　　　　63
Brand colour Quiz Answers　　　　　　　　　　　　65
About The Author　　　　　　　　　　　　　　　　67
Thank you for your purchase　　　　　　　　　　　69

"A business is the body and brain. A brand is the heart and soul."

— ALEX WILLIAMS, FOUNDER OF ALEX WILLIAMS DESIGN

INTRODUCTION

Hello. I'm Alex Williams, a freelance graphic designer specialising in brand identity design for small businesses. I've been working as a graphic designer since 2008, and in 2020, I took the leap to set up my own business.

As a graphic designer and passionate business owner, I know what a BIG deal it is to get something as important as your brand spot on. It needs to 'speak 'everything about your business, its values and its purpose. And that's what I'm here for. I love helping small businesses improve their brand and showcase their amazing products or services, which ultimately contributes to their business growth and success!

I've helped lots of small businesses level up their brand by:

- Helping them find clarity in their business
- Creating stand-out brand assets which align with their vision and personality
- Giving them confidence to show up and show off their amazing businesses

Not all start-ups have the budget to work with a brand identity designer, which is why I've created this guide to help small business owners with little to no budget create their brand. I understand it can be overwhelming starting a business from scratch (I've been there) and if I'd had some sort of brand guide at the beginning, I know it would have helped me. My specialist skills lean into the more visual side of branding, but I also have plenty of experience in marketing and business. So, in this book, you'll find lots of helpful info about all the aspects of building a strong brand.

What is a brand and why is it different from a business?
A business typically provides goods or services in exchange for profit, whereas a brand is the identity, personality and perception of a business. A business *could* operate without a brand, but having a strong and well-managed brand helps:

- Connect the business to its ideal customers
- Create a professional image
- Make the business stand out
- Extend the brand with consistency
- Help customers understand what the business is about
- Encourage enquiries and sales

You *can* create your own brand
Brands are not just for big businesses. The aim of this book is to help you (as a small business owner or entrepreneur) create a strong brand without overcomplicating it – and on a minimal budget! You can refer to this book time and time again, whilst you build your brand.

"If people believe they share values with a company, they

will stay loyal to the brand."

— HOWARD SHULTZ, FOUNDER OF STARBUCKS

I've put the chapters in order of what I'd start with first, but it's not essential you follow the order. You can totally dip in and out of each section. There's a handy checklist at the back too – you can also find a free printable version on my website, which you can satisfyingly check items off once you've completed them!

OK, intro over, let's jump straight in…

CHAPTER 1 – NAMING YOUR BRAND

Who is your brand?

One of the main reasons I wanted to write this book is because I often get asked *what should I name my brand?* It's such a big decision and when you don't feel you have the right name, it can stop you from moving forward. But if I could give you one piece of advice, it'd be this… **don't get too hung up on it**.

Go with your gut. Worst-case scenario, you change it. (People do.) Did you know Amazon started out as Cadabra. Inc.?! Even my own business started off as Sweetsmith Designs!

That said, here are a few ways to help you conjure up a name.

Use Your Name

This is a great option for freelancers, solopreneurs and anyone who wants to be the face of the brand. But this isn't limited to those who work alone. Using your name is the easiest and quickest way to get your business up and running. Your friends and family aren't exactly going to say *I don't like that name.* So, if you're someone who likes to keep things simple, this option might be for you!

A big benefit of naming the business after yourself is that it's quicker to get your name out there when you're starting out.

You are the business and, as a newbie, you'll want referrals coming in. So, when you're networking, introducing yourself or telling people about what you do/offer, it'll be easy for people to remember you and your business – as it's the same name.

Instead of using your name, you could use the name of a family member, a friend or even a pet!

Big brands that use their names: *Coco Chanel, Kate Spade, John Lewis, Dyson, me! (Alex Williams Design)*

Use A Word That Describes Something Your Business Does

If you like the idea of giving your audience a clue about what your business does, you could include a word linked to your offering. It's a great way to add personality but still give your audience an idea of what you do. You can have fun with this, and it can also help with search engine optimisation.

Big brands that include what their business does in their names: *Just Eat, Mailchimp, The White Company, Pizza Hut*

Use Words That Aren't Associated With What You Offer

When all the obvious names have already been taken for your product or service, and you don't want to use your name, consider using a random word (or words). It could be as simple as your favourite colour plus your favourite animal, e.g. Pink Cat or Pink Cat Designs.

Big brands with names that aren't associated with what they offer: *Red Bull, Caterpillar, Amazon, Apple*

Use Made-Up Words

If you can't (or don't want to) use random words, then how about making up a word? The good thing about this is that your name is going to be unique. Just be mindful of having to communicate how the name is pronounced and that the word isn't offensive or means something derogatory in a different language.

Big brands that use made-up words for their names: Kodak, Rolex, Pixar

Combine Words, Or Parts Of Words, To Create A New Word (A Portmanteau)

This is a mix of the two previous options, where you combine words that describe what your business does to make a new word (a portmanteau). Netflix (net + flix) is a great example of a portmanteau, with 'net 'representing the internet/streaming (how you use their service) and 'flix', an alternative spelling of 'flicks', which is slang for the cinema. Netflix – a made-up word – is now synonymous with watching TV/films. Netflix and chill, anyone?

Big brands that use portmanteaus for their names: Instagram (instant camera + telegram), Pinterest (pin + interest), Snapchat (snap + chat), PayPal (pay + pal)

Use An Acronym Or Initialism

A good way to shorten a long name and make it memorable is to use an acronym or an initialism. Acronyms form "words" from the first letter of each word, for example NASA. Initialisms are where you sound out the first letter of each word, like IBM (I-B-M).

Big brands that use acronyms or initialisms for their names: DPD (Dynamic Parcel Distribution), ASOS (As Seen On Screen), NERF (Non-Expanding Recreational Foam)

Use A Location

You could use the location of your business as inspiration for your brand name. Street names, towns, part of the postcode or even something more general such as 'Sea View 'could all work well for your business. You'll notice bars and restaurants do this.

Big brands that include a location in their names: *KFC (Kentucky Fried Chicken), Adobe (Adobe Creek), Cisco (San Francisco)*

Use Words With A Hidden Meaning

I love brand names that aren't obvious where they originated from but have meaning behind them.

Big brands that have a hidden meaning in their names: *Five Guys (named after the owner's five sons), LEGO (an abbreviation of the Danish leg godt, meaning "play well")*

Try A Play On Words

If you want to inject some humour into your brand, you could consider using a pun. Classic examples are 'Curl Up and Dye' for a hairdresser or 'The Codfather ' for a fish & chip shop. I can't actually think of any big brands that do this, which speaks volumes. When you piggyback off something like a film or a song, you risk infringing on copyright – so be careful!

However, I couldn't resist including some examples to make you smile:
- Bread Pitt
- Thai Tanic
- Tequila Mockingbird
- Lord of the Wings
- Surelock Homes
- Lino Richie

- The Rolling Cones
- Tree Wise Men

Naming Top Tips

Name generating

If your mind is blank or you just can't think of a good name for your brand, here's a technique which is quick, fun and gets results!

You'll need:
A big piece of paper
A pen
A timer

Method
Set the timer for ten minutes and write down as many names/ideas that pop into your head. No overthinking. Just let the creativity flow and write, write, WRITE until the time is up.

Then highlight the ones that stand out and that you think could work. Sometimes, jotting down random words sparks ideas you wouldn't have ever otherwise thought of.

This is also a great activity for involving friends, family or team members!

Name Checking

Once you've decided on a name, write it down – with no spaces – to make sure it doesn't spell anything offensive.

Trademarks

You may want to work with a trademark specialist, who can check the name you've chosen is OK to use.

Your Brand Name Does Not Need To...

Tell the whole story of your business, be too literal, or be restrictive.

CHAPTER 2 – BRAND PERSONALITY

How do you want your brand to feel?

Figuring out your brand's personality might not seem important, but I'm going to tell you three ways how it can improve your business…

- **Differentiation** – Having a distinct brand personality helps you stand out from the competition.
- **Emotional connection** – Brands with a well-defined personality can evoke emotions and build deeper connections with their audience.
- **Brand loyalty** – Brands with a well-defined personality tend to attract loyal customers who are passionate about the brand's values.

Now you're either thinking *brand personality – pah! What mumbo jumbo is that*? or, *I can't wait to discover my brand's personality.*

The key word here is discover! By discovering your brand's personality, you will be able to understand your business better and create content more easily, which will result in more effective marketing and, ultimately, more sales.

Here are the three ways I would go about trying to define your brand's personality:

1. What words describe how you

want your brand to feel?

This is something I ask my clients, to help me work out what vibe they're going for. If a business owner wants their business to feel a certain way, they can use their brand personality to differentiate it from their competition.

I'll use a hair salon as an example. You could have two hair salons in the same town, but they're both completely different. One aspires to be a luxury hair salon aimed at busy females who want some time out to pamper themselves. The other salon is aimed at families. The first salon might want their brand to feel luxurious, exclusive and calming. The second salon might want their brand to feel playful, accessible and cool. Without giving you much information, I bet you can understand how these brands would feel completely different.

Exercise

Here's a list of describing words to help get you started. I would recommend circling 3–5 words you would want your brand to be associated with. You might think, well, I want my brand to feel all those things, but try to select only 3–5, to force you to pick the most important words.

- Approachable
- Authentic
- Beautiful
- Bold
- Collaborative
- Cool
- Creative
- Different
- Diverse
- Eco-conscious
- Educational
- Elegant
- Exclusive
- Family friendly
- Fashionable

Feminine
Friendly
Fun
Happy
Healthy
Helpful
Innovative
Intelligent
Kind
Luxury
Masculine
Natural
Positive
Professional
Quality
Real
Relaxed
Reliable
Rustic
Secure
Sensual
Simple
Unique
Vintage
Wise

2. Brand archetypes

Brand archetypes are universally recognised personas that a brand associates itself with to create a distinct identity and connect with its target audience on a deeper, emotional level. This concept was popularised by Swiss psychologist Carl Jung, who identified archetypes as fundamental human symbols and themes that are present in myths, stories and dreams. Marketers have adapted Jung's ideas to create brand archetypes as a way to shape and communicate brand personality.

There are several common brand archetypes, with their unique characteristics and appeal. You can create your own mix by choosing three archetypes that you (and your brand) feel most connected to.

The Hero
Hero brands convey courage, strength and overcoming obstacles. Brands aligned with the Hero archetype focus on triumph and achievement.

The Innocent
Innocent brands symbolise simplicity, purity and nostalgia. They appeal to goodness and wholesomeness.

The Explorer
Explorer brands are adventurous and encourage their customers to be the same. They promote freedom and self-discovery.

The Sage
Sage brands represent wisdom, knowledge and expertise. Brands aligned with the Sage archetype position themselves as authorities in their field.

The Lover
Lover brands are passionate and sensual. They focus on desire, intimacy and connection.

The Jester
Jester brands are playful, fun and light-hearted. They use humour and entertainment to engage their audience.

The Caregiver
Caregiver brands are nurturing, compassionate and empathetic. They position themselves as protectors and providers.

The Creator
Creator brands are innovative and imaginative and often seen as artists or visionaries. They encourage creativity and self-expression.

The Ruler
Ruler brands are authoritative, powerful and often associated with leadership and control. They convey a sense of order and stability.

The Everyman
Everyman brands are relatable, down to earth and appeal to the average person. They focus on inclusivity and community.

The Outlaw
Outlaw brands are rebellious, unconventional and challenge the status quo. They appeal to people who want to break free from norms.

The Magician
Magician brands are transformative and focus on wonder and possibility. They tend to emphasise the power of change.

What's Your Unique Mix?

Archetype	Archetype percentage (make total to 100%)
1.	
2.	
3.	

For example: My brand identifies as 40% Jester, 40% Creator and 20% Everyman.

3. Personality slider

A brand personality slider includes a set of contrasting personality traits or characteristics on opposite ends of a scale. I use this with my clients to help them visualise how their brand might sit on a sliding scale of each contrasting quality. A brand might want to feel luxury, but when it comes down to answering *how* luxury, they might not be sure. They might discover they're high end rather than super luxury. Hotel Chocolat is a luxury chocolate brand that is more expensive than, say, Cadbury's or Galaxy, but it's still affordable to most. It's perceived to offer luxury chocolate, but still be accessible. A designer brand such as Louis Vuitton, however, offers luxury products with a much higher price tag, putting them in the super luxury category and unaffordable to the general consumer.

You can access my brand personality slider via my website. by clicking here. Think about your brand and place a dot on each row of the slider. You could also ask friends, colleagues or customers to mark out where they think your brand sits on the personality slider to see if they're aligned.

Fun exercise

Now if all that was a bit overwhelming, here's an exercise that requires less brain power.

Did you know that using the right emojis can strengthen your brand? Using emojis is a creative and visual way of conveying the traits and characteristics that your brand embodies. Emojis are widely recognised symbols that can quickly communicate emotions, values and attributes.

Select emojis that align with the personality traits you want

people to associate with your brand.
- ☐ A smiling face suggests your brand is friendly and approachable.
- ☐ The lightbulb emoji symbolises innovation and creativity.
- ☐ Stars suggest your brand stands out.
- ☐ The rainbow stands for diversity and inclusivity.
- ☐ The trophy represents achievement and success.

A mix of emojis can help communicate your brand's unique personality and values.

So, for my brand, I use the following emojis:

☐✍☐☐

- The iMac shows my business involves a lot of digital work.
- The drawing hand suggests creative work.
- The heart conveys my brand is warm and friendly – I want my brand to feel welcoming.
- The sunglasses give off a fun, cool and relaxed vibe.

Why don't you type out some emojis for your brand and write why you chose them or what they represent. As well as obvious ones (such as an ice cream if you're an ice cream shop), try to select some that sum up your unique selling point or personality.

Emoji	Reason
1.	
2.	
3.	
4.	

Now you have your brand personality established, you can use it

ALEXWILLIAMS

to help extend your brand and keep it consistent.

CHAPTER 3 – BRAND VALUES, MISSION AND VISION

Why do you do it?

Your brand's mission is what your brand is doing right now. It's beyond the obvious *to make money* and is a more personalised statement. Your brand values are the beliefs that you, as a company, stand for and are meaningful to your brand. Your vision focuses on the ultimate destination and what your company hopes to become.

Your brand values are the core principles and beliefs that underpin your brand and define its character. Think of them as your brand's ethical and moral compass.

Your mission statement is a concise explanation of why your brand exists, what it does and for whom. It outlines your brand's purpose and primary objectives.

Your vision statement describes your brand's future or long-term aspirations. It paints a picture of what your brand hopes to achieve in the years to come.

Let's revisit those two hair salons to visualise how their values and their mission and vision statements could be different. I've also included some potential emojis for them.

Salon 1's brand values: luxurious, calm, beautiful, feminine.

Salon 1's mission statement: To provide a calm and luxurious experience where busy females can escape their daily lives and leave feeling refreshed, with beautiful hair.

Salon 1's vision statement: To be a sanctuary of self-care for busy, empowered women. We understand the demands of modern life and aim to create a haven where our clients can escape the chaos, rejuvenate their spirits, and leave feeling confident and radiant.

Salon 1 potential emojis: 🍃💁‍♀️✨🤍
- Green leaves to represent calm.
- Hair flick to represent good hair and confidence.
- Stars to represent luxury and glamour.
- White heart to represent peace and elegance.

Salon 2's brand values: fun, cool, friendly, inclusive.

Salon 2's mission statement: To provide a fun experience where families can get cool hairstyles without having to worry about making too much noise!

Salon 2's vision statement: We aspire to be the go-to family hairdresser, through creativity, self-expression and togetherness.

Salon 2's potential emojis: ✂️⚡👨‍👩‍👧‍👦🤪🌈
- Scissors to represent hair cutting and creativity.
- Lightning bolt to represent trendy vibes and excitement.
- Family to represent it being a family-orientated salon.
- Silly face to represent fun.
- Rainbow to represent inclusivity.

Want A Stand Out Brand?

This is often the priority when rebranding. Business owners want their brand to stand out against the crowd. But how do you do that? Hint: it's not having an all singing, all dancing logo. If you figure out your brand's values, mission and vision and have your visuals aligned to these; that's when you'll create a stand out brand.

With all the foundations supporting the visuals you'll have a stronger brand and *a brand with meaning.* Take some time to think about your values, mission and vision.

Your brand values *(what words do you want associated with your brand?)*

Your brand's mission *(who you help, how you help them, why you help them)*

Your brand's vision *(the future for you brand – what are you aiming for?)*

Now you can see what's important to you and what your business stands for, it will make marketing – and strengthening – your brand easier.

CHAPTER 4 – TARGET AUDIENCE

Who is it for?

Please don't say *everyone*. Seriously, please don't say everyone. Your business should not be targeted at everyone. That doesn't mean you need to exclude people from using your services, it just means you should identify your ideal audience – the people you aspire to connect with most. When you tailor your branding to resonate with this specific group, you increase the likelihood of attracting the people who are most inclined to purchase from you.

Defining your target audience can be daunting when you're just launching your business. It's challenging to predict who will purchase from you without any prior sales. I totally get it, because I've been there. I did not have a clue who my target audience was when I first started out. So, if you're like me and don't know right now, that's OK because you will eventually figure it out. Once you get a few sales under your belt, here's what you can begin to analyse:

- What type of people enquired?
- Where were they from?
- What gender were they?
- What age range were they?
- Do they belong to any specific professions or industries?
- What did they buy from you?

- What are they into?
- Where do they hang out?
- What's their favourite TV show?
- What are their pain points and challenges?
- What are their goals and aspirations?
- What social media platforms do they use?

The answers to these questions will reveal insights about your audience. You'll begin to notice patterns and similarities, which will allow you to identify the types of individuals who are drawn to your offerings. Once you've collected this data, you can create a buyer persona to represent your customer base, which will help you tailor your marketing towards that typical customer.

Some businesses segment their offerings because they recognise that one group of people might prefer one service, while another group prefers another. The approach you take can vary; you might opt for separate website sections, distinct social media accounts, or even choose to focus exclusively on one service while discontinuing another. There's no definitive right or wrong way – it's how you want to grow your business.

How My Business Evolved

When I launched my business, I offered a wide range of graphic design services. Given my strong background in graphic design and my love for logo design and branding, it was an obvious choice to prominently feature logo design as one of my services. I also love illustration, although my experience in the illustration industry is pretty limited. Nonetheless, since I was actively creating digital illustrations for social media at the time, I decided to include illustration services in my offerings. And because I'm fond of typography prints, I then added those to my repertoire too.

Consequently, I was providing an array of services tailored to both businesses (business-to-business) and individual customers (selling typography prints). As you can imagine, defining my target audience proved to be a challenging task. I had enquiries from businesses looking for branding solutions, larger businesses wanting one-of-a-kind illustrations, and orders from families interested in my prints. Maintaining a consistent social media presence was a struggle because I was uncertain about the type of content I should be sharing. It felt disjointed, and I recognised that I might have confused my customers.

After careful consideration, I divided my business into two distinct parts. One would specialise in brand identity design, while the other would focus on bespoke illustration and prints. I created separate websites and social media platforms. I dedicated most of my time and energy to brand identity design and planned to assess the viability of continuing with illustration after a year of being in business.

Once I narrowed my focus, it was clear to see who my target audience was and how I could help them. My messaging and marketing became easier, and I started to get consistent enquiries as clients could see what I offer and how I get results. It's approaching two years since I did that, and it is the best business decision I've ever made. The illustration side of the business has been put on hold for the time being – I just couldn't manage to keep up with both. However, I would love to pick it back up again in the future. I think we need to be realistic with our time and what will make our businesses viable.

Narrow Your Focus

If you have multiple services or product lines you want to streamline so you can figure out your target audience, here are some questions to help you decide what to focus on.

Service-based businesses	Product-based businesses
What projects do you like working on?	What are your best sellers?
What projects do you feel most drawn to?	What product would you use yourself?
What types of clients do you like to work with?	Do you often get requests for anything else?
What industries do you prefer working with?	Which products are you proud to show off?
What type of enquiry excites you?	What types of customers do you enjoy engaging with?
Does this work come easy to you?	Is this easy to make/get hold of?

When you narrow your focus and start talking to your target audience in a way that resonates with them, your brand messaging and marketing becomes much easier.

CHAPTER 5 – SERVICES/PRODUCTS

What do you do?

This might seem obvious, but it's so important to define (and frequently communicate to your audience) what services and products your business offers. Your brand personality, values and target audience can help filter and streamline the products and services you offer.

If we go back to the hair salon example (in Chapters 2 & 3)…

The haircare products and services the first salon offers would be quite different to what you'd find at the second salon. The first salon might want to stock high-end, luxury haircare products and offer a glass of complementary champagne on arrival. The family-friendly salon, on the other hand, might want to stock cool merchandise, brightly coloured hair wax and perhaps have an in-salon gaming area to entertain bored kids!

If you want to open a hair salon and have no idea what your brand's personality should be, or you haven't defined your target audience, then it'll be harder to define and refine the services and products you'll offer.

Keep It Simple

Don't make your services unnecessarily complicated or your

product line too random – it'll put up a barrier and put customers off making the final purchase.

Start Small

You might have dreams to offer multiple services and hundreds of products, but when you're a new business, it's a great idea to start with a small selection of products or a minimal service offering so you don't confuse or overwhelm your audience. Have you ever visited a restaurant where there's just too much choice on the menu? If you're like me, you'd rather have a carefully curated menu with six main course options rather than a list of a hundred which are all very similar.

What's Your Core Offering?

When you have a core service or product, it's much easier to market that one thing. You can talk about that service or product in much more detail, which helps your audience understand what you offer.

Benefits Of Having A Core Service Or Product

- You'll become known for offering that thing!
- You'll be seen as an expert or the go-to business.
- Previous clients will be able to easily explain what your business offers.

Tips To Help Define Your Core Services

- What are you most passionate about?
- What could you talk about confidently without any prior preparation?
- What service does your target audience need?
- What service do you have the most experience with?

Tips to help pick your core products
- What do you think will be your bestseller?
- What product do you know how to use inside out?
- What products would you like to have yourself?
- Would you use/eat/wear this product yourself?
- Is this product a trend?
- What product do you believe would help your customers?

Niching

Let's take a few minutes to talk about niching. I feel like people either love or hate it! If you haven't heard of niching before, it's targeting a specific segment of the market with specialised products or services. Instead of trying to appeal to a broad audience, businesses focus on meeting the unique needs and preferences of a niche market. This can lead to increased customer loyalty and a competitive advantage in that specific market segment.

I love niching. It's helped me so much in my business! I concentrated on one core service within the graphic design industry (brand identity design) and niched to offer brand identity design to small businesses at the start-up or level-up phase of their business. This really helped me focus my marketing on that specific target audience.

Here are some examples of industry niches.

Standard business	Niche business
Hairdresser	Hairdresser who specialises in rainbow hair colours
Car repair	Audi repair specialist
Business insurance	Business insurance for photographers
Yoga instructor	Yoga instructor for over 60s
Cake maker	Kids novelty cake specialist
Florist	Wedding florist for rock 'n' roll brides

Business owners often think if they limit their business services, they'll get less customers, but then find the opposite – they become a specialist or the go-to person (or business) for their niched offering and, therefore, stand out in a crowded marketplace.

Niching is not essential and it's not for everyone. Some people like to be generalists, and that is perfectly OK! And don't niche because you think you have to. If you don't want to offer (for example) rainbow hair, then I wouldn't recommend niching for the sake of it. You've got to find a niche that aligns with your passions and beliefs.

Unique Selling Point

A Unique Selling Point (USP) is something that makes a product or offering stand out and gives customers a clear reason to choose it over others. It highlights what makes a business or product unique and valuable, making it more attractive to potential customers. A compelling USP attracts the attention of your target audience, drawing them towards your product or service. It can pique curiosity and generate initial interest. A USP can be a big thing, like stocking only ethically made products, or a small thing, like offering a free mystery cookie with every coffee purchased before 11am.

Some Examples Of Great Usps

Domino's
"We GUARANTEE – Fresh hot pizza, delivered in 30 minutes or less or it's FREE!"

McDonald's Happy Meal
The famous low-cost children's meal has been available since

1979 and is still as popular as ever. No matter where you are in the world, if you find a McDonald's, you know you'll be able to find a child-friendly meal!

IKEA
IKEA offer high-quality furniture at low prices, with the convenience of having it selected, assembled and in your home by the end of the day, even on a whim.

To figure out your USP, ask yourself:
What does your business do well? And what does your customer want?

When defining your products and services, play to your strengths, evaluate what works and don't overcomplicate it!

Find Your Usp

To figure out your USP, ask yourself: What does your business do well? And what do your customers want? Why don't you list some things you know you or your business can do well. Then list some things you know your customers want. If you don't know what they want, ask them! Ask them on social media, ask them in person, contact customers who've purchased from you. When you have a list for both, think about what two you could combine to create your USP?

What your business does well	What your customers want

CHAPTER 6 – VISUAL IDENTITY

What do you look like?

This is the meatiest chapter of the book and rightly so – it's my specialist area! Your visual identity is all the parts of your brand that you can see: logos, colour palettes, fonts and any patterns or icons. The whole identity should be aligned to your brand, meaning that everything you've picked from your fonts to your colours matches the vibe you're going for.

Choosing mismatched colours or fonts can let your brand down and confuse your customers. Imagine having the wrong fonts or colours. It's a bit like being invited to a posh ball and wearing jeans and a T-shirt. There's nothing wrong with jeans and a T-shirt, but they just aren't right for the occasion! In this chapter I'll give you tips on picking the best colours, logos and fonts for your brand.

Colours

Picking colours for your brand can be harder than you think! But as it's such an important part of your visual identity, it's worth spending time on getting it right. If you don't have a professional logo or visual identity set up, you can use consistent colours to help establish your brand.

When I work with small businesses, I tell them to think of

one or two colours they want their brand to be associated with. You can definitely have more than two colours, but picking and using two main ones will help establish your brand and make it recognisable. Did you know that 95% of the world's biggest brands only use one or two colours in their logo? If you think of some of the biggest brands in the world, you'll probably visualise their brand colours immediately.

Think of the following brands – what colours come to mind?
(Answers at the back of the book)

1. McDonald's
2. Starbucks
3. Facebook
4. IKEA
5. Coca-Cola
6. Spotify
7. Marvel
8. Nickelodeon
9. Google
10. PayPal

Successful brands know that using the same colours over and over creates brand recognition. Brand recognition makes it easier for brands to be remembered and to stay top of mind.

Real-life example
I was walking to the local shop with my children, and we saw a bus stop in the distance. The advert at the bus stop was Cadbury's – I could see their famous purple background and make out the shapes of the glasses of milk. I asked my children if they could see what the advert was. Straight away, they both said Cadbury's. An eight year old and a ten year old instantly recognised the colour and thought it must be a Cadbury's advert. That's the power of being consistent with brand colours.

Picking colours
How you want your brand to look and feel will depend on what

colours and ratios you use. For example, if you want to have a light and airy brand, you might want to use light colours such as white and neutrals. But let's say you want a really vibrant, high-energy brand – then, you might want to use bright, highly contrasting colours. You might also want your brand to include bright colours without them being in your face, in which case you could use lots of black and white and then have bright colours dotted throughout.

Top tips to picking your brand colours
Choose about five colours for your brand:
- 1 dark neutral (black, dark grey, navy, dark brown, etc.)
- 1 light neutral (white, cream, light beige, light grey, etc.)
- 1 main accent colour (the colour you want your brand to be known for – this could be one of your neutrals by the way)
- 1 or 2 optional accent colours used sparingly throughout your brand

If this is still too complicated or overwhelming, simply pick two colours and use them consistently.

Logo Design

As a graphic designer who's been working in the design and marketing sector since 2008 and who has designed more than 25 professional logos since going freelance, I'd like to think I'm experienced and know what I'm talking about when it comes to logos!

Your logo is often considered the most important part of your brand and whilst I do kind of agree with that, it's not the only thing that matters when creating your brand.

Do I need a professional logo?
If you're considering opening a physical store, where signage and packaging play a significant role, I'd strongly recommend investing in a professionally designed logo right from the

beginning. Having a quality logo is essential for making a positive and lasting impression.

However, if you're a start-up with a substantial digital presence, you might be able to delay getting a professional logo and rely on other visual elements, such as photography, social media, and the growth of your online following through product showcases and user-generated content.

If you don't have the budget to work with a professional graphic designer, here are your options:

- Do it yourself using Canva or an alternative.
- Use a free or low-cost online logo generator.
- Find a designer on Fiverr.
- Ask a student or friend to help you.

If you're thinking of designing your logo yourself, here are some top tips to make it look as professional as possible:

- Make sure your business name is readable.
- Make sure your business name is the most prominent part.
- Make sure it works in your chosen colours, but also in black and white.
- Don't include any special effects.
- Don't use a font that you love but that doesn't work for your brand.
- Create variations for different-sized spaces.

Fonts

Fonts convey the personality, tone and values of your brand, so choose them carefully. Before you do, have a clear understanding of your brand's personality and values. Is your brand modern and innovative? Traditional and reliable? Playful and friendly? Or something else entirely? Your font choices should align with these characteristics.

Consistency and appropriateness in font selection are crucial. When a font doesn't match the brand's intended message or target audience, it can lead to confusion and even drive potential customers away. I visited an upmarket restaurant whose food sounded really lovely, but whose font choice made the menu look really cheap. It was jarring, and the restaurant missed an opportunity to convey their high-quality cuisine through their typography.

Most frequently used font types and what they are suited to
Below is a guide to common font types and their typical uses. While these are general guidelines, keep in mind that design rules can be flexible and creative. But if you're not experienced in design, this can be a helpful starting point.

Font type	What it conveys	Industry examples	Where they can be used
Serif	Traditional, timeless, reliable	Luxury brands – timepieces, fragrance, high-end fashion	Logos, headings, sub-headings, body copy
Chunky serif	Retro, bold, welcoming	Fun brands, alternative brands	Logos, headings, sub-headings
Lightweight sans serif	Minimal, clean, neutral	Make-up, skincare, minimal fashion, creatives	Logos, headings, sub-headings, body copy
Bold sans serif	Bold, statement	Bold fashion brands, sports, musicians	Logos, headings, sub-headings
Slab serif	Masculine, industrial	Trades	Logos, headings, sub-headings
Monospaced	Utilitarian,	Computers/	Logos,

		typewriter effect	tech, coffee shops	headings, subheadings, code
	Calligraphy	Luxury, relaxed	Luxury brands, weddings, beauty	Logos, headings, sub-headings
	Handwritten	Fun, creative	Children's toys/ accessories, art brands	Logos, headings, sub-headings

Fonts Vs Typefaces

A **typeface** is the family of fonts e.g. Helvetica, Times New Roman, Futura.
A **font** is the specific variation of that typeface e.g. Helvetica Bold, Times New Roman Italic, Futura Condensed Medium.

Typography

Typography is the art of arranging type (letters, numbers and symbols) to make written language legible, readable and visually appealing. When I started my graphic design degree, we were taken to a typography department, which had lots of typography examples pinned up on the wall. I remember thinking *how is this art or design? It's just words on a page*. Ah, how little did I know back then!

There is a lot involved in creating simple and readable text. Interestingly, it's often easier to identify poor typography than it is to recognise good typography. Poor typography can be visually jarring and give off an unprofessional vibe.

If you want to create your own documents, here are some tips to

keep your typography looking good:

- **Hierarchy** is essential in design as it prioritises information and ensures effective communication. For instance, your primary message or headline, often referred to as the hook, should be more prominent than your secondary or detailed information. Similarly, your call to action (CTA) can be bold or highlighted, but it shouldn't overshadow the main title. When the text receives equal prominence, there's nothing to capture the reader's attention, and the content might appear as a monotonous block of text. To engage your readers and create visual interest, establish a clear hierarchy that guides their focus.
- **Font choice** – First, ensure you choose fonts that align with your brand's identity. Second, limit how many you use.
- **Breathing space** – Providing sufficient breathing space or white space for your text is essential as it helps focus the reader's attention and enhances readability.
- **Don't squeeze** – Avoid overcrowding text on a single page and refrain from aligning it too closely with the margins.
- **Body copy** – For the main text (the body copy), use either a sans serif or a serif font. Anything else will be too hard to read in large amounts.
- **Consistency** – Once you have decided on your hierarchy, fonts and layout style, be consistent to ensure a professional and polished typography style.
- **Alignment** – Choose the appropriate alignment (left, right, centre or justified) for the context. Left alignment is standard for most text, while centre alignment is often used for titles.

Other Visuals

Patterns and illustrations

Creative elements such as patterns or illustrations can really add a playful edge to your brand's identity. Illustrations can elevate information, so it's definitely worth considering if you want to add personality to your brand.

If you're using Canva (or an alternative) to create graphics for your brand, you might come across templates which include pre-set patterns or illustrations. These are fine to use, but make sure you choose elements that suit your brand's identity. You should be able to change the colours and remove any elements you don't want to use.

Photography
Good photography can totally lift your brand. I see people getting this so wrong when trying to build their brand. But it's crucial you either improve your photography skills or hire a professional. A good product can look really bad if you don't get the photography right.

Hiring a professional photographer is worth its weight in gold. However, if you simply do not have the budget for this, when it comes to photographing your product, you need to think about quality over quantity. It's not that difficult, it just needs a little thought.

Here are my top three tips for capturing a great photo:
- **Lighting is key** – If you're taking photos indoors, wait for the time of day when the light is best or invest in a ring light.
- **Move clutter out of the background** – sounds obvious, but unwanted extras can spoil a good photo.
- **Try different angles** – close-ups, full-length shots, shots from above – just experiment.

Service-based businesses can be harder to photograph, in which case I would strongly recommend hiring a professional photographer to capture you/your team at your office, or, if you work from home, at a location that suits your style.

Another option would be to use stock photography, which is widely available online. Whether you opt for free or premium stock photography, there's so much that's easily accessible that you should find something suitable for your brand. This is a great way to access professional photography without much effort. The only downside is that it lacks your brand's unique stamp and other companies could be using the same images. It also tends to look quite generic, so take some time to pick stock photography that suits your brand.

The key to getting your visuals right is quality and consistency. Don't be tempted to share average graphics or photos in the hope that it generates interest and sales. Always give a good impression to build a strong brand.

CHAPTER 7 – CONSISTENCY

Help them remember you

Consistency is the absolute key to creating a professional and recognisable brand. Your goal should be to maintain uniformity and coherence in all aspects of your brand's identity, your messaging, and your communication across your channels and touchpoints.

Why You Should Be Consistent

Builds trust with your audience
When your brand is consistent in its messaging, visual identity and values, it shows that your brand is reliable and dependable. If your business offers a high-ticket service, this should be your main priority.

Improves recognition
Consistency makes it easier for your audience to recognise your brand across your channels and touchpoints. This is important because it creates brand recall, which can increase the likelihood of your brand being top of mind when someone needs your product or service.

Establishes credibility

Consistency establishes credibility for your brand. By consistently delivering a high-quality experience and maintaining a consistent visual identity and messaging, your audience will perceive your brand to be professional and trustworthy.

Helps you be unique
In a crowded market, consistency helps your brand stand out. When you maintain a unique visual identity, messaging and values, you can differentiate your brand from your competitors. The more authentic you are, the harder it will be for your competitors to replicate what you do.

Ways To Be Consistent

Use consistent colours and fonts
I see inconsistent colour and font use so often, and it really pains me! I understand businesses may not have a visual identity set up, but picking colours/fonts and being consistent with them is such an easy way to establish your brand and gain trust.

Use templates
Creating templates that include your chosen colours and fonts will keep your brand consistent and save you time. Types of templates you could make include:
- Menus
- Price lists
- Presentation slides
- Social media templates (Instagram posts, Instagram Stories)
- Website hero graphics
- Notices

Imagine if you had no templates, and every time you needed to communicate something to your customers you had to create documents from scratch. Now imagine you have templates set up, with the colours and fonts already added. All you need to do is concentrate on the information you want to share. You can use free platforms such as Canva or Adobe Express to create templates.

Use the same tone of voice in your messaging
If you've established your brand's personality, then you can use a tone of voice (TOV) that aligns with how you want your brand to feel. Be consistent with your TOV so your customers resonate, and become familiar, with how you communicate.

Communicate what your business offers
You may think your customers know what products or services you offer, but you need to be reminding them. And whilst it's good to evaluate and develop your business, you also need to be mindful you're not constantly changing your offering – and confusing your customers.

Consistent marketing
I'll go into marketing in more detail in Chapter 9, but for now just know that consistent marketing is much more beneficial than bursts of marketing activity when you're quiet. Be realistic about the time you have available and dedicate that time to a few marketing outlets.

3 Quick Tips To Become More Consistent

Save templates into folders
Label each folder and create duplicate files so as not to overwrite the original template.

Organise your photos into folders on your phone
It may take an hour or so to set up but, believe me, organising your photos and videos into folders will save you so much time when you're looking for content for social media.

Schedule generic posts
Schedule posts which include information that doesn't change very often, such as services or price lists, so there's a consistent drip of information going out to your audience.

CHAPTER 8 – CLAIMING YOUR SPACE

Helping them find you

Now you've established the foundations of your brand and have set up your visuals, you need to carve out a space for your brand so customers can find you. Here are three things I recommend doing to claim your space…

Register Your Business On Google

Registering your business on Google is really easy, and I don't understand why more businesses don't use this free marketing tool. It's good for local SEO, it makes your business look professional and it's another place where customers can find you. Plus, if you start collecting reviews via Google, you're going to build trust with your audience.

Claim Your Domain

Even if you don't plan to have a website straight away, it's still a good idea to claim a domain name as closely matched to your brand name as possible. You can pick one up for around £10 (it'll be renewable annually). So, when you do decide to have a website, you'll have a domain ready and waiting. Plus, it stops anyone else buying it before you.

When you buy your domain, you can add a custom email address, such as info@yourbusinessname.co.uk or hello@yourbusinessname.com. Some businesses continue to use their free email address to avoid unnecessary cost, but I think that cheapens their brand. While using a free email address is acceptable for personal use or small projects, it's generally advisable to invest in a custom domain email address for your business to enhance professionalism, credibility and trust among your audience. The relatively small cost of a custom domain email service is well worth its benefits in building a strong online brand presence.

Instagram

If you're planning on using Instagram for your brand, you'll also want to grab an Instagram handle. There are so many social media platforms out there, but Instagram is one where your handle matters.

Your Instagram handle is your account name, and it's what people can tag you as on their posts, reels and stories. Since Instagram currently has 1.3 billion users (at time of writing), there's a high chance the name you want has already been claimed, therefore you might have to get a bit creative.

Let's say you run a bakery and you've named yourself The Cake Stop, but @thecakestop has already been claimed. You might then want to consider @the_cake_stop or @the_cakestop_bakery.

There are lots of combinations you can try. You can't use spaces, so I'd recommend using underscores to break the words up. You can use full stops, too, but I think underscores look better. You can also use them at the end of the name like this: @thecakestop_

I wouldn't advise using numbers at the end of your name because it will look like a personal account, or a little cheap.

By doing these three things, you can help customers find your business. Now it's time to tell the world about your brand!

Get Listed On Directories

Find directories that are relevant to your industry and see if you can be listed on them. Some will be free – I'm part of a freelance network where my information and services are
displayed. Can't find a directory? Create your own! Think about businesses who aren't a direct competitor, but complement your brand. E.g. If you were a wedding cake maker,
you could set up a local wedding suppliers directory on your website – imagine the increased traffic you'd get from all the suppliers sharing the link. You can also pay a fee to
be listed on more premium directories – usually websites where they already have a high amount of traffic.

Networking Groups

Some networking groups only allow one business per industry, so sometimes there can be wait lists for really popular networking groups. If you have your eyes on joining a particular one, then enquire as soon as possible.

By doing these things, you can help customers find and trust your business. Now it's time to tell the world about your brand!

CHAPTER 9 – MARKETING

Telling people what you do

Don't be scared by the word 'marketing'. On a very basic level, marketing is telling people that your business exists and what it offers. If you only do the very basics, you're still marketing!

Of course, there is a lot more to it than just the basics, but because I don't want to overwhelm you, I'm going to list some easy ways to get started on marketing your business!

10 Ways To Market Your Business Without Being Completely Overwhelmed

1. Tell your friends and family.
2. Add your business to a relevant directory.
3. Use social media.
4. Join Facebook/WhatsApp groups.
5. Post flyers locally.
6. Networking.
7. Begin email marketing.
8. Write press releases.
9. Write blog posts.

10. Collaborate.

Marketing

I'm now going to dive deeper into three that work for me and are probably a good three to get started with.

Social Media

Social media is brilliant. It's free (mostly). You can share whatever you're doing with anyone in the world. It's great for meeting people, sharing ideas, sharing your business and more... with no boundaries. However, the popularity of social media has made us rely on it, and a lot of new business owners put ALL their marketing efforts into social media and social media alone. And whilst you might grow quickly on social media, you've got to remember that things can change at any time.

Quick validation

I often hear business owners say they aren't getting many likes or views on their content and it's a waste of time. They feel disheartened that they've spent a lot of time creating content only for it to 'flop'. One business owner told me he deleted posts after an hour if they hadn't achieved a certain number of likes because he thought it was bad content! It's such a shame we rely on this instant validation to determine whether our content is good enough. When you stop going after the number of likes, and instead work on an overall marketing plan, you will achieve so much more.

Going viral

People are also under the impression that if you go viral or get lots of likes and engagement that it'll be easy to run a successful business. That's not true. I've seen small accounts with videos that go viral – small accounts that are shared by celebs and influencers – but they don't necessarily grow. Yes, they get a ton of new followers, but that doesn't translate to long-term, consistent sales. In fact, my own Instagram account has been shared by huge accounts, and I get very little back. Don't focus on going viral. Focus on a consistent message targeted to your ideal target audience and then *if* a piece of your content does go viral, it might transfer into lots more new followers because they'll resonate with the information you've already shared.

Let's look at the pros and cons of the main social media platforms.

Social media platform	Pros	Cons	Considerations
Instagram	Friendly community. You can build a loyal following.	The algorithm seems to constantly change, which can be frustrating.	Aesthetics do matter – use appropriate posting sizes. Requires preparation.
TikTok	Each post has the potential to reach billions of users, so you can grow your account quite fast.	Users tend to have less of a filter, so be prepared for negative comments.	Using TikTok can be liberating as you can try out different types of content to see what works for your brand.
Facebook	If you already have a personal account, you can share your business page	Older generations and community groups tend to use this, so it	Try setting up or joining a private group in your industry or

	easily to your friends and family.	might not suit a forward-thinking brand.	niche.
LinkedIn	Your content has the potential to reach new audiences quite quickly, especially those in higher positions.	Can feel more business-like, which won't suit everyone. Expect cold sales pitches dropping in your inbox.	Start by adding your friends and family and your network will grow.
Twitter/X/Threads	Quick and easy to post, no need to prepare graphics.	Can be limiting for creatives.	Great for writers and comedians who have a way with words!
YouTube	Great hub for video content. YouTube offers the opportunity to earn money through ads and partnerships.	To stand out, it might take a lot of effort and professional video editing skills.	Success on YouTube often requires a thoughtful approach. Lots of adverts.

It's best to choose one or two social media platforms you're comfortable with, rather than trying to have a presence on them all and spreading yourself too thinly. Avoid lazily copying and pasting your content from one platform to the next. Instead, repurpose your content so it's better suited to each platform.

To sum up, social media is worth considering for marketing your business. It's free (unless you choose to run ads), it's easy to set up, you can run all your marketing from your phone, and there's plenty of support and tips available from experts.

Email Marketing

Marketing experts often advise you build a mailing list. Once you've collected email addresses, you can choose what you want to do with them (following GDPR guidelines of course). You don't have to worry about an algorithm changing or your account being blocked. Once you have the emails safely stored, you can communicate directly to those interested in your service. It takes time to build a mailing list, so don't be disheartened if you don't have a huge list. Just remember that if someone gives you their email address, they have shown interest in your product or service. Email marketing therefore gives you quality leads at your fingertips, as opposed to posting to thousands of potentially uninterested people.

The great thing about email marketing is that you can set up automations so that when people sign up, the platform automatically sends out welcome emails and more. There are much more advanced features, such as audience segmentation and A/B testing, but even for sending out regular emails and promotions, it's worth spending time setting up and creating content regularly.

There are plenty of email marketing platforms available, most of which offer a free basic package sufficient for most start-ups. Popular platforms include Mailchimp, ConvertKit, MailerLite, HubSpot and any built into your website. I use MailerLite as I find it really easy to use and customise.

Networking

Networking, whether in a professional or social context, offers a wide range of benefits including:

Opportunities for collaboration
Networking connects you with individuals and organisations that may share common interests or goals. This can lead to valuable collaborations, partnerships or joint ventures.

Knowledge sharing
Networking allows you to tap into other people's knowledge and expertise. You can learn from their experiences, insights and perspectives, which can be valuable for your personal and professional growth.

Enhanced visibility
Being visible and active in your network can help build your personal or professional brand. This can lead to increased recognition and credibility in your field.

Business growth
For entrepreneurs and business owners, networking can generate leads, new clients and referrals. It can also lead to partnerships and opportunities for expanding your business.

Networking can be very daunting when you've just started a business, especially for introverts. If you don't know anyone at a networking event, it takes a lot to enter a room and potentially start talking about yourself and your business to absolute strangers. I've been there – and still go to networking events where I don't know anyone. However, the more you do, the more you'll start to see familiar faces, and it's great for building up local connections.

Top tips for networking newbies

- Wear something you feel confident and comfortable in.
- Get there early so that you're one of the first to arrive. It's easier to start conversations with one or two people than it is

entering a busy room full of people already in conversation.
- Hang around the coffee station, then people will naturally come towards you.
- Have a purpose for attending the event to get more out of it.
- Smile.

Businesses prefer to work with other local businesses, especially if they have been recommended by friends and colleagues. So even if you go to a networking event and feel like you didn't collect many leads or contacts, someone may well go on to recommend you. There are loads of networking groups/events up and down the country. Go to a few to see which ones you get the most out of.

General Marketing Tips

Did you know?
The marketing rule of 7 states that a potential customer needs to see a message at least seven times before they'll be moved to take action. Seven times! So don't think you can post one picture on social media and your job is done.

Being consistent – real-life example
I follow a fashion influencer on Instagram, who quite often shares beautiful, but pricey, trainers. Every time she shares them, I swoon. I really want them, but I know I can't justify buying them right now. The thing is, when I do need a pair of trainers and I'm ready to invest, all it will take is for the influencer to share them when I'm in the right frame of mind and it'll be a done deal. But let's flip this… let's say the influencer only shared the trainers once and I'd only seen them once. Yes, I might have fallen in love with them right away, but if I wasn't in the right frame of mind to buy them, I'd likely forget about them. The key is to warm people up with consistent marketing. Marketing can be instant, but generally you need a plan in place that involves regularly sharing information about what you do, who you are, who you serve, etc. to consistently generate leads and sales.

Content pillars

I'll finish this chapter with content pillars and how they can help you with your marketing strategy. A marketing strategy just means a marketing plan. It's good to have a bit of a plan, rather than just stabbing in the dark. So, here's an easy way to work out what content you should be creating:

First, think about **what you want to be known for**? And **who you want to be known to**?

For example, I want to be known for helping small businesses build a strong brand in a fun and easy-to-understand way.

Then think about what kind of information you'd need to share, to help the people you want to be known to.

For me to help small businesses improve their brand, I need to:
- Share branding tips (actionable)
- Explain basic graphic design and marketing (educate)
- Provide creative inspiration (inspire)
- Talk about small business life (relatable)

Some more examples…

Type of business	Known for	Known to	Content pillar examples
Coffee shop	100% vegan coffee shop	Vegans and those with dietary requirements	Benefits of being vegan (educate) Sharing vegan recipes (educate/actionable) Showcasing the coffee shop (sales) How the business is making a change (inspire)
Electricia	Specialised	Parents	Sharing quick

n	in helping busy families	with little knowledge of electrical safety	safety tips (actionable) Explaining basic electrical terms (educate) Before and after transformations of new lighting etc. (inspire/sales/community) Communicating flexible working times and punctuality (reassure)
Make-up studio	Providing natural beauty looks	30+ females who want to enhance their beauty	Sharing skincare tips (actionable) Make-up demos/reviews (entertain/educate) Before and after transformations (inspire/sales) Customer journey from booking to arriving at the salon (reassure)

If you're not sure what the people you want to be known to want from you, think about frequently asked questions you receive and turn these questions into content pillars.

Marketing is much more than selling. In fact, sales should only make up about 10% of your content. You will get much more traction from sharing a mix of tips, educating your audience and helping them through your content rather than constantly selling.

10 Quick Marketing Tips

1. Brainstorm ideas every month.
2. Re-purpose old content.
3. Check analytics to see what's working.
4. Invest in working with a marketing expert.
5. Something not selling? Try a different approach. Sometimes people just need the information presented differently for it to make an impact.
6. Keep an eye on trends, but don't get too caught up on them.
7. If you feel burnt out by the thought of creating content – take a break.
8. Remind yourself of your customers' pain points and communicate how you can help them.
9. Over communicate benefits of the product or service you're selling.
10. If you're really stuck just make sure your content answers at least one the following: who, what, where, why, when, how.

CHAPTER 10 – CUSTOMER SERVICE

Your reputation

Now you're starting to make sales, you need to look after those customers to keep them coming back and turn them into loyal followers. You also need to welcome new customers.

Keep Up To Date

Regularly check the information on your website and social accounts is up to date and links are working. There's nothing worse than seeing out-of-date information on a website. I've seen restaurants with the previous year's Christmas menu still on their website in June. Just as you wouldn't leave your Christmas lights up all year, remove seasonal promotions as soon as possible after the event has passed.

Offer An Easy Customer Journey

A customer journey is the different stages in which a customer finds your business and then goes on to make a purchase or enquire. You want to make the journey as streamlined as possible, with as easy, few steps as possible, so they are more likely to complete the enquiry or check-out process.

Make Contact

A marketing expert once told me not to have too many contact options. You'd think that having multiple contact options would be a good thing. However, if you give your customers too many options, they then have to make a choice – which is an extra decision. Choose your preferred contact choice and make that prominent on your website/social media.

Do What You Promised

This may sound completely obvious, but if you said you were going to provide a service/get back to a customer/ship a product by a certain date, do it. Missing deadlines does not bode well.

Communicate Clearly

Sometimes things happen beyond our control. If something is delayed, communicate that to your customer. If something has gone wrong, don't try to cover it up. Admit it and provide a solution.

Collect Reviews

Reviews are a great way to build your reputation and build trust with potential customers. Reviews can also provide you with content ideas (a bit like FAQs).

Embrace Feedback

Encourage customers to provide feedback and use this information to make continuous improvements in your products and services.

Keep Consistent

Consistency provides reassurance to customers. So make sure your visuals are consistent to keep building on that trust.

Don't Be A Robot

You can be both professional and offer a glimpse into the more personal side of your business. You could show 'day in the life' videos or behind the scenes content. If you have employees, you could show some interesting information about each team member or have photos of groups of staff on your website. Photos of animals always do well :-)

Handle Complaints

Turn negative experiences into positive ones by addressing complaints with empathy and finding solutions that satisfy the customer.

Real-Life Examples

A negative experience
I use a piece of software which helps me run my business smoothly. I don't utilise the software to its full capacity, but I rely on one particular feature.

Recently, there was a glitch with the software – resulting in me not being able to use my favourite feature for at least a week while the IT department fixed it. As I could still use the software in some capacity, I didn't feel I had the grounds to complain. However, after I waited patiently for them to fix the issue, I asked the company if they'd be willing to discount my next bill. To which they replied no.

I thought it was a little blunt, but accepted it. However, after some thought, I actually felt really annoyed that they couldn't offer me a small discount, say 10% off my next bill, as a gesture of goodwill and to keep a loyal customer happy. Ultimately, I decided to cancel my subscription. I went through the cancellation process and the usual steps… are you sure you want to cancel? Please don't leave us etc and continued with the cancellation, until at the final stage they offered me 90% off my next two bills. 90%!! I welcomed the huge discount and I continued with my subscription, but despite the large discount I just wished they'd acknowledged the inconvenience in the first place.

A positive experience
A few years ago I ordered a Christmas tree from an online retailer at the beginning of the December of that year. I received a confirmation email, followed by an email to say it had been dispatched. However, a few days later I received another email saying that the product was now out of stock and they would let me know when it would be back in stock
and out for delivery. Naturally this worried me that I'd be without a Christmas tree, but I waited patiently. As the days crept closer to Christmas Day, it was obvious I wasn't going to
have a nice new tree and would have to settle for the old tree (with the half broken lights) and just buy a new one much earlier next year.

In the new year I phoned customer services to get a refund. They instantly issued me with a refund which was a quick and easy process, but what surprised me was that they also said that because I'd waited so patiently and that because they'd let me down that they would also give me a gift card and still let me have all my store points. It probably didn't cost a lot for them to do this, but that gesture made me feel like my waiting and stress was acknowledged without prompt, which showed
empathy. It's difficult to judge where to draw the line sometimes when it comes to complaints, but if you've let your customer

down – a small gesture can go a long way. It builds the trust back up – which is so important if you want to retain your customers.

SUMMARY

After reading this book, you'll hopefully understand how having a strong brand has the following benefits:

- Provides an identity
- Creates brand recognition
- Establishes trust
- Connects your business to your ideal customers
- Creates consistency
- Makes marketing easier
- Increases sales
- Drives long-term success

If you take time to build your brand with intention and make sure everything is aligned, you'll build a brand that lasts.

Further Help

I hope you've enjoyed reading this book and that you'll take away some information to help establish or improve your brand. If you feel like you need further help to strengthen your brand, then please get in touch with me to see how we can work together.

Contact me via my website
www.alexwilliamsdesign.co.uk/contact
Follow me on Instagram
www.instagram.com/alexwilliams_design

CHECKLIST

- Choose your brand name.
- Check Instagram to see if your handle is available.
- Check to see if your domain name is available.
- Select 3–5 words to describe how you want your brand to feel.
- Pick 4–6 emojis to represent your brand.
- Decide on your tone of voice (TOV).
- Write your brand values and mission and vision statements (this is an ongoing process).
- Define your target audience.
- Work out your core services.
- Create your unique selling point (USP). What do you want to be known for?
- Create a logo.
- Lock in a colour palette (write down your colour codes).
- Select fonts to match your brand's vibe.
- Design some templates to save you time and help you be consistent on social media
- Book a professional photographer.
- Or download stock photography that matches your brand's vibe.
- Register your business on Google.

You can also download a printable version of this checklist here

BRAND COLOUR QUIZ ANSWERS

1. McDonald's – Red & yellow
2. Starbucks – Green
3. Facebook – Blue & white
4. IKEA – Blue & yellow
5. Coca-Cola – Red, black & white
6. Spotify – Green, black & white
7. Marvel – Red & black
8. Nickelodeon – Orange & white
9. Google – White & primary colours
10. PayPal – Two shades of blue

ABOUT THE AUTHOR

Alex Williams

Alex Williams is a graphic designer and founder of Alex Williams Design – brand identity design specialist.

Alex has over 15 years of design and marketing experience and has worked with hundreds of small businesses.

Alex is based in the north east of England and especially loves to help businesses local to her, but also has had clients world wide!

Passionate about art and design in general, you'll often find Alex doodling in her sketchbook or looking for inspiration in nature and the world around her.

THANK YOU FOR YOUR PURCHASE

If you enjoyed this ebook, it would mean the world to me if you could leave me a review on Amazon.

www.ingramcontent.com/pod-product-compliance
Lightning Source LLC
Chambersburg PA
CBHW070358230526
45471CB00006B/2621